This Annoying Life
Oslo Davis

Black Inc.

Published by Black Inc.,
an imprint of Schwartz Publishing Pty Ltd
37–39 Langridge Street
Collingwood VIC 3066, Australia
enquiries@blackincbooks.com
www.blackincbooks.com

All illustrations by Oslo Davis.

Printed in Australia by Griffin Press. The paper this book is printed
on is certified against the Forest Stewardship Council® Standards.
Griffin Press holds FSC chain of custody certification SGS-COC-005088.
FSC promotes environmentally responsible, socially beneficial and
economically viable management of the world's forests.

This book is for Minami and Yuna,
my very unannoying daughters.

Introduction

Some things never change. More than two and a half millennia ago the Buddha told us that life is suffering, and lo and behold, it still is! Sure, there's lots of pleasant things in life (like the laughter of children, a puppy tripping over his paws, or that first pull on a cigarette after twelve hours on a bus, for example), but by and large there's still lots of annoying stuff.

And I'm not talking about the big annoying stuff like cancer, wars or Senator Cory Bernardi. I'm talking about the small stuff that we all sweat every day. The niggly little perturbances that get on our nerves. The minor disturbances that ruin everything, set us back a few paces and take us down a few pegs. You know what I'm talking about. Like when the beautiful young woman ahead of you in the queue is laughing with the barista instead of ordering a coffee. Or how it takes you a few goes to pull yourself up and out of a pool. How you can never find the end of the sticky tape. How it's virtually impossible to get the hot/cold balance right in the shower. How in the middle of the night you realise that a CD you lent to a friend four years ago hasn't been returned. And how you sometimes yawn too wide and nearly lock your jaw.

This Annoying Life is a book of stuff we all have a hate–hate relationship with. While you may enjoy the images here in a kind of schadenfreudey way, this book is also an invitation for you to return to a childlike state and colour them in. (Who cares what your friends think!) It offers you a chance to clear your mind and open a path to mindfulness, whatever that means. At a bare minimum *This Annoying Life* will help you find your way back to a new you that you've never met before but have heard a few things about, not all of them bad.

In conclusion, I'd like to butcher a quote by Thich Nhat Hanh, the author of *Peace Is Every Step: The Path of Mindfulness in Everyday Life*, who famously said 'Walk as if you are kissing the earth with your feet', by saying 'Colour in as if you are kissing your annoying life with pencils'. You could do a lot worse.

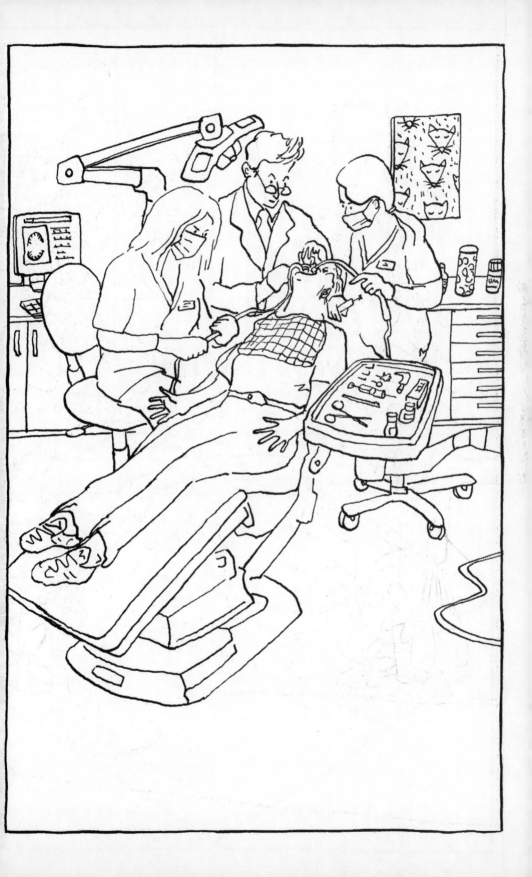

3:45 AM

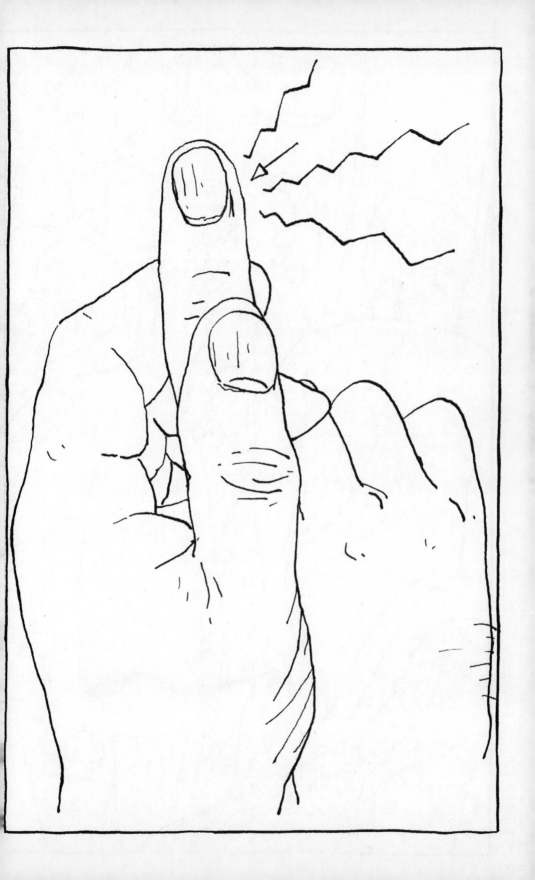

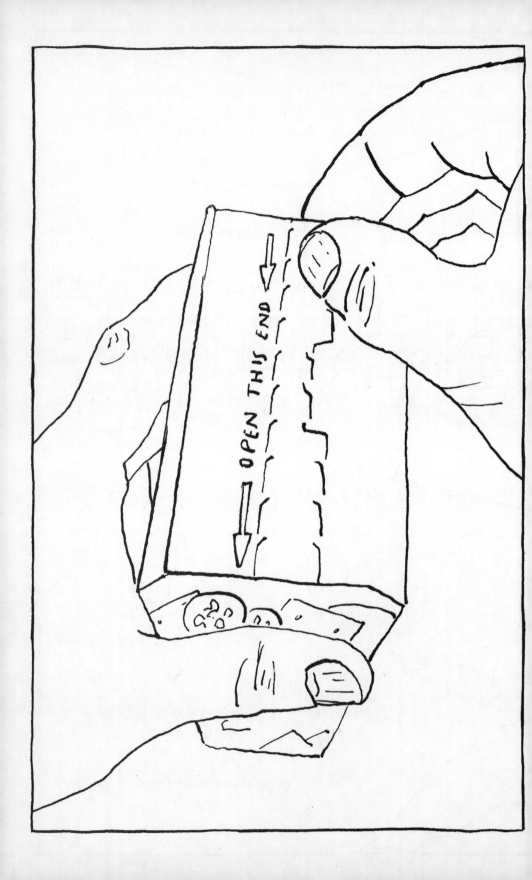

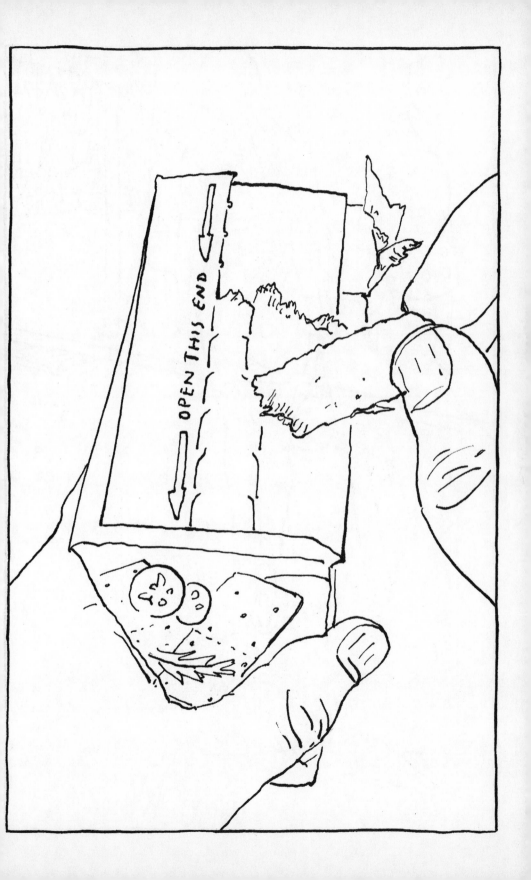

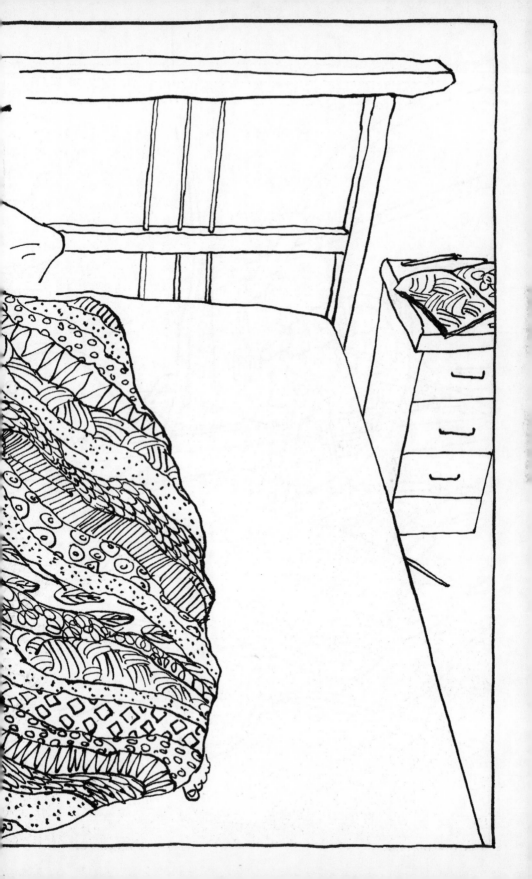

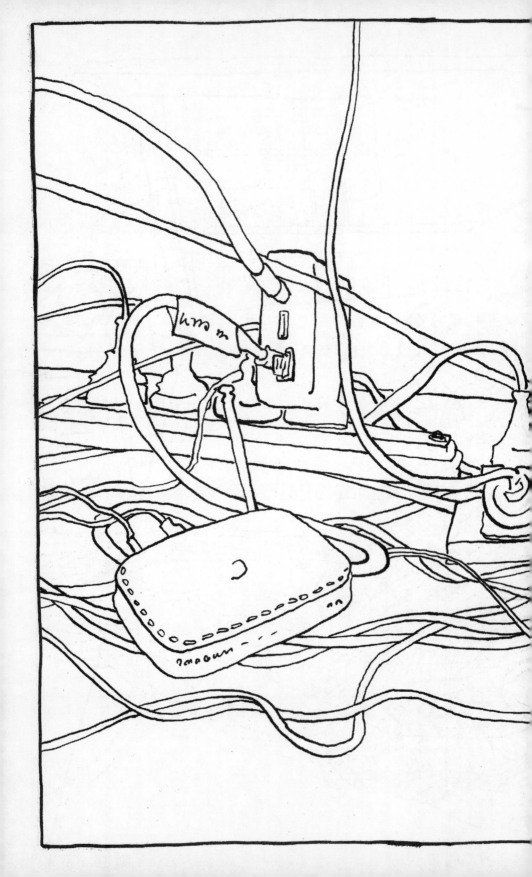

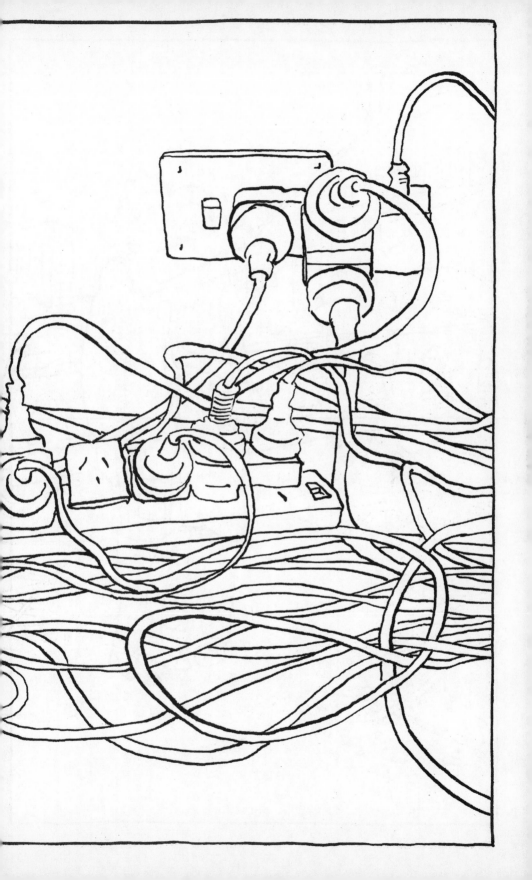

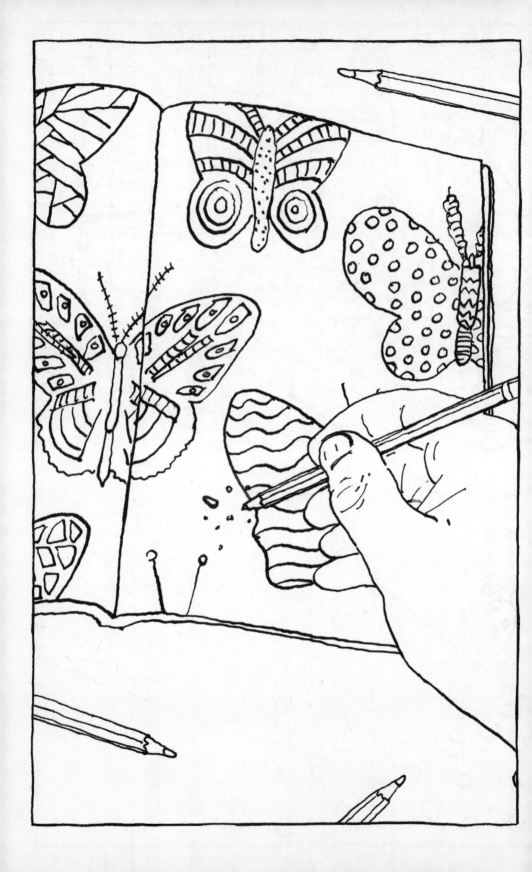

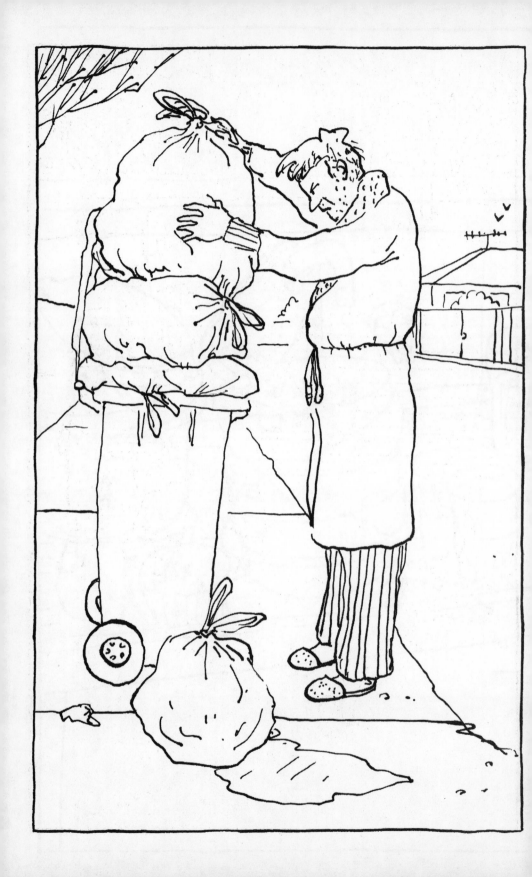

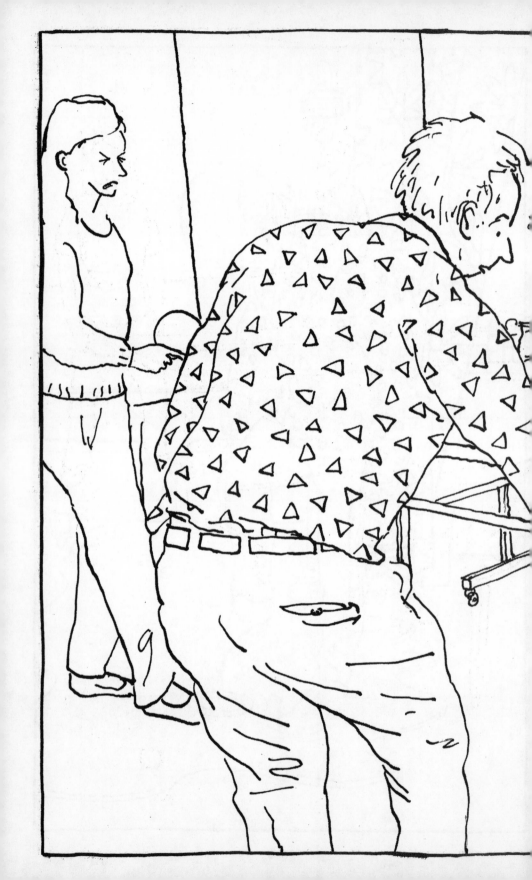